In my vision at night I looked, and there before me was one like a son of man, coming with the clouds of heaven. He approached the Ancient of Days and was led into his presence.

Daniel 7.13

ONE LIKE A
SON OF MAN

JESUS AND THE KINGDOM IN MARK'S GOSPEL

RICHARD C. GEORGE

The way of
THE SPIRIT

Published in Great Britain by The Way of The Spirit, Norfolk, UK

www.thewayofthespirit.com

First edition published July 2022

Second edition printed April 2023

The Way of The Spirit is a charity registered in England and Wales, number 1110648

ISBN 978-1-9085-2871-1

CONTENTS

ACKNOWLEDGEMENTS

I thank God for all those who played a part in bringing this course to fruition. For those who attended the 16 Zoom sessions during that first lockdown and the team who supported me each week and made it happen. For those who advised, suggested and edited: Patricia Napier, Carol Holland and Catherine Ayre; for Hedley Quinton and the Resources team, and for Men Gei Li and Annette Schittenhelm, the PAs who kept production moving forward. And for the prayer team—for the work done in the hidden place.

Thank you everyone for your encouragement, practical skills and suggestions and thank you Lord for providing the best.

PREFACE

I didn't always find Mark exciting. It was when I listened to teachers who took the Kingdom of God seriously that it began coming alive. My impression had been that the 'Kingdom' was something distant and theoretical—maybe a synonym for the church. The Gospels however show that Jesus taught the Kingdom as something imminent and concrete, quite distinct from the church. As I began to grasp this, Jesus' life and ministry as related in the Gospels became compelling.

The expression of the Kingdom of God seen in Jesus' ministry in the three years or so before his final journey to Jerusalem forms a crucial aspect of the Gospels. It is not just the cross that is important. Yet in 20 years of church life the significance of this had somehow eluded me. It was only as I listened to the teaching of John McKay, Colin Urquhart and others that the Kingdom began taking its proper place in my thinking.

The more I saw, the more I could put into practice, and the more I put into practice, the more I saw. Theory became reality and history became exciting. Where I had previously viewed Biblical characters through historical and cultural filters, I now saw them as men and women who—like me and so many others—had one way or another encountered God. I also saw with increasing clarity how Jesus did not appear in a vacuum but rather in fulfilment of a long history of relationship between God and his people. In this light it was not just the Gospels but the whole Bible, from Genesis to Revelation, which came alive and inevitably led back to, and illuminated, Jesus and his Kingdom in Matthew, Mark, Luke and John.

Jesus also spoke much about faith, and I began learning from the Gospel accounts how faith operated in and around him. I began to consume teaching from men and women who were themselves learning to apply the faith they had been given to seeking first the Kingdom. 'Come, follow me!' Jesus had said, and I heard him say it afresh to me, as if for the first time. An adventure began which has been variously exciting, fruitful, awful, miraculous, terrifying, thrilling and desperate—just as it was for Jesus and his followers.

Constrained to do only his Father's will, Jesus was also a follower, and thus modelled what it means to walk by faith, seeking first the kingdom. Or—as Paul aptly describes it—serving in this 'new way of the Spirit'.[1] The way Jesus walked, as described for us in the Gospels, thus becomes our road map and provides the sharpest expression of God's Kingdom and how to live as his disciple. For me, learning to prioritise walking in obedience and faith began to replace every religious or super-spiritual instinct in me that wanted to default to something else—something that might look good but which would be a poor substitute for stepping out and trusting him.

Later the Lord led me to university, where further study of the Gospels added another dimension to my understanding. In the decades since, through following Jesus and seeking to equip followers of Jesus, I have taught and trained men and women in many countries. Each time, I receive more revelation—often even as I stand teaching—and that in turn always enhances my own journey. What a joy it has been!

---

[1] Romans 7.6

During Covid lockdown, in early summer 2020, God spoke to us in The Way of the Spirit: 'Go, prophesy again!'—echoing his command to John in Revelation Chapter 10. Rather than lean into an enforced time of rest and recuperation (which no doubt would have been extremely pleasant) we began teaching Mark on Zoom in weekly sessions of 45 minutes. It took 16 weeks to finish Mark, and we collected numerous regular listeners. God was graciously giving fresh revelation and the Holy Spirit was moving. We saw people greatly encouraged and built up—sometimes even physically healed during the sessions. The Holy Spirit moved across continents in front rooms, back rooms and bedrooms—wherever they had access to Zoom.

It is this set of audio sessions which, apart from the Biblical text of Mark, form the centrepiece of this study. The notes set out here in 16 parts correspond to the audio teaching, and the questions bring some of the main points home, allowing you to think about how to apply the teaching.

I pray you will receive life as you listen, read and stretch to complete the study each week. It may prove not for the faint-hearted—though will be eminently accessible, I trust, to all who seek to follow Jesus and know his Kingdom better.

HOW TO USE THIS WORKBOOK

This course can be enjoyed by anyone, no matter how much or little prior understanding of Mark's Gospel they have.

Completing this study will:

- inspire you with a fresh revelation of Jesus, the Kingdom and how both relate to you today;

- enable you to understand one Gospel—its broad structure, themes and own particular way of expressing Jesus and his ministry, death and resurrection;

- give you clear understanding of the significance of Jesus' three-year ministry before the cross, as well as the cross itself and its aftermath;

- strengthen your faith and teach you about how it operates in the Kingdom and in relation to Jesus;

- provide deeper understanding of how Jesus came to fulfil the purposes of God related in the Old Testament;

- help equip Bible teachers, providing a solid foundation on which their own lifetime exploration of the Gospels can be built;

- feed your spirit with God's truth in the power and anointing of the Holy Spirit.

Mark is the shortest Gospel, containing less teaching than Matthew or Luke, and having no details of Jesus' life prior to the beginning of his ministry. It is therefore an ideal place to begin a study of the Gospels.

There are FOUR components to the study:

- The BIBLICAL TEXT. (You will need your own Bible—quotations are taken from the NIV unless indicated otherwise.)

- The AUDIO RECORDINGS 1-16.

  - Recordings can be downloaded free of charge from:
    www.thewayofthespirit.com/son-of-man-audio

    OR

  - You can buy them on a USB stick from the web shop at
    www.thewayofthespirit.com/son-of-man-usb

- The written NOTES 1-16. These are in this workbook and correspond to the audio recordings.

- The QUESTIONS 1-16. These follow the NOTES.

Use the different materials in any way you wish. Some may not wish to engage much with the written notes, preferring only to listen to the audio teaching before answering the questions. Others will relish both the audio and the notes. Whatever else you do, I would urge you always to read the Biblical text each week and always to attempt the questions.

The most effective way to use this course would be to study one section per week in a group of 2-8 people. In this case each group member should listen to the relevant week's audio recording during the week prior to meeting together. They may find it equally effective to listen to it as they meet together, though this will limit the time available for discussion. Alternatively, like other The Way of the Spirit courses it can still work well when studied alone.

Each audio recording is about 40 minutes long. Come to it prayerfully and expecting to receive life (not mere theology), and sometimes the theological content may thrill you. Always ask yourself how to apply what you are learning and invite the Holy Spirit to help you. One of his jobs, after all, is to 'lead us into all truth'.

The Gospel can be divided into five (unequal) sections. We have colour-coded each, which will help you navigate your way through the whole book (see diagram below). The first section—the introduction—is what Mark tells the reader but which the characters in the narrative are not party to. A little like the overture in an opera, it sets the scene for the action which begins properly at Jesus' baptism at the Jordan. Section two—the longest—is Jesus' Galilean ministry: Jesus bringing, teaching and demonstrating the Kingdom, making impact among the people away from the Jewish leaders in Jerusalem.

The third section is the journey Jesus undertakes with his disciples and others from Galilee to Jerusalem to face the authorities there. The fourth section describes Jesus entering Jerusalem and all the events there leading up to the cross, and the final section beyond to the resurrection and his appearances to the disciples.

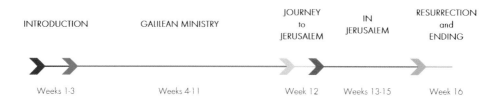

INTRODUCTION	GALILEAN MINISTRY	JOURNEY to JERUSALEM	IN JERUSALEM	RESURRECTION and ENDING
Weeks 1-3	Weeks 4-11	Week 12	Weeks 13-15	Week 16

The biggest rewards will come not in beginning this study but in finishing it! Commit to completing the course and get to know Mark's Gospel in its entirety.

❯ INTRODUCTION

• 1

THE BEGINNING OF THE GOOD NEWS

MARK 1.1 - 3

I invite you to put aside all you already know about Mark's Gospel. Come with fresh eyes and watch Jesus confront sickness, death, demons, wind and storm, then turn away from his revival ministry towards Jerusalem and the cross. This narrow way of obedience will ultimately lead him into the very presence of his Father, to be seated at his right hand. Consider, as you read through the Gospel week by week, what it means for you to follow Jesus— to be his disciple today.

Just as we might today read the back of a paperback to see what it is about, so readers in Mark's time could have read the opening lines of a scroll to see what it contained, and here they would have read: 'The beginning of the good news about Jesus the Messiah...'[2]

So what is the beginning of the good news? That after 400 years without any recorded prophetic or other spiritual activity in Israel, John the Baptist now bursts onto the scene heralding the arrival of Jesus. Israel's history as recorded in the Old Testament is replete with individuals empowered with God's Spirit. We recall, for instance, Samson slaying thousands with a

---

[2] Mark 1:1

donkey's jawbone after the Spirit of God came upon him,[3] and Samuel under the influence of the Holy Spirit prophesying with his band of prophets.[4] This good news is an account of Jesus, the Anointed One (variously translated as Christ or Messiah, both meaning one anointed with the Spirit of God), called and equipped by God with the same Holy Spirit for a timely and specific ministry: to operate in the power of that Holy Spirit, and to inaugurate the age of the Kingdom.

During his lifetime Jesus makes no explicit claim to be the Messiah or Christ, but instead allows his life and ministry to speak for itself. The rather dim disciples will take a long time to catch on, seemingly struggling to understand, yet somehow managing to follow anyway, sometimes hanging on by their fingernails, at least until Jesus' last days when fear will overtake most of them and they will flee.

Mark sets the scene by reminding us of certain prophetic words uttered many years before, for their fulfilment will be seen in Jesus' ministry. Like many things Mark writes in his Gospel, these fulfilments aren't spelled out but are discovered by those who can read between the lines. He begins telling us about the good news by quoting from Isaiah 40.3 and Malachi 3.1.[5] If we want to fill in the gaps between the lines, we need briefly to consider the context of each, for they will illuminate the action that is about to take place.

---

[3] Judges 15.14-15
[4] 1 Samuel 19.20
[5] Mark 1.2-3

First, Mark 1.3 (from Isaiah 40.3). The people of Judah had been exiled from their promised land and carried off to Babylon where they would spend nearly 70 years. Despite the many words God had sent, this was something they had never believed would actually happen to them. Surely they were God's chosen people, occupying God's promised land? But God had warned them over and over again about turning to other gods and their practices and he is always true to his word. After all, he had once told King David very clearly that though his love would never be taken away from his descendants, if they did wrong he would punish them with a rod wielded by men.[6] That punishment was now upon the people of Judah.

Isaiah's words comforted the people of Judah as they were marched off to Babylon. Despite the now unavoidable exile, they were reassured that God's words remained true. 'Comfort, comfort my people! Tell them their sins have been paid for. God has not abandoned you to your fate, people of Israel! One day a voice will again call in the wilderness … prepare the way of the Lord … and the glory of the Lord will be revealed, and ALL PEOPLE everywhere will see it—not just Israel—for God has spoken![7]

Israel at the time of Jesus was still waiting for the fulfilment of these promises, though of course many had long ago stopped looking for God to break in again, for they had lives to live and other things get on with. Their ancestors had returned from exile 400 years previously but the devout, at least, were still waiting for that voice in the wilderness to signal a new move of God in their land and beyond. In other words, Mark was using Isaiah to remind us

---

[6] 2 Samuel 7.14
[7] Isaiah 40.1-5 (Author's interpretation)

that Israel was still waiting for the day when a voice would be heard that would prepare them for a new move of God in their nation. This move would lead to his glory being seen again—this time not only by those in the land but by all people everywhere.

The Isaiah and Malachi prophecies remind us of different aspects of God: set apart, different from us, holy. Furthermore, reading on in Malachi[8] we find the Lord coming in judgement, as a refiner's fire. Yes, God's glory would come again, but it would not be at the expense of his righteousness and holiness.

---

[8] Malachi 3.2-4

QUESTIONS

1. **Mark 1.1–3, Isaiah 40.1–5, Malachi 3.1–4.**

    Compare the coming of the Lord as described in Isaiah 40 with that in Malachi 3. How does the glory of God relate to his holiness?

2. Imagine you were with the people being carried off into exile. How would Isaiah's words in Chapter 40.1-5 have resonated with you? What promises would you have seen in them, and how would you have expected to see them fulfilled?

3. Have you personally ever felt that God's words and promises to you have come to nothing? Explain.

4. Why does Mark open his Gospel with these scriptures? Why are they 'the beginning of the good news'?

5. 'For the mouth of the Lord has spoken' (Isaiah 40.5c). What is the significance of this statement? Do you have words that you know for sure God has spoken to you?

• 2

TURN BACK TO GOD AND BE READY FOR WHAT HE IS ABOUT TO DO

MARK 1.4 - 8

Imagine that there has been no evidence of the presence of the Holy Spirit in our churches for four hundred years: no prophetic activity, sense of God's presence, Spirit-led worship or revelation from the preaching and Bible reading. No wonder the religious system in Jerusalem is dry and legalistic as John is about to launch his ministry.

Though we read about John in the New Testament Gospels, from his prophet's garb to his calling for repentance he is in many ways more reminiscent of the Old Testament prophets. His entire life's work and purpose has been to point to Jesus; for this he was conceived and born. His life has been spent in preparation for a brief season of drawing large, attentive and hungry crowds, alerting them that God is about to break in again to their nation and to the world, and calling them to repent in order to be ready for what he is about to do. John has no desire to draw the crowds to himself; everything he does is to direct their attention to Jesus who will soon follow.

John tells the people: 'The one who comes after me will baptise not in water but in the Holy Spirit! The man of the Spirit, whom I live to serve, will immerse you in a baptismal pool full of God; you will come out dripping not water but God (for the Holy Spirit is God). And then, in the power of the Holy Spirit you, like me, will have the opportunity to spend your life pointing others to Jesus.' (Author's interpretation)

It is fascinating that in the opening eight verses of his Gospel, as Mark summarises the ministry of Jesus, he says nothing about the cross but instead emphasises Jesus' mission to baptise in the Holy Spirit. The cross is of course crucial to Jesus' ministry—the fulcrum on which the whole of history pivots. We can see here, however, that Mark considers it to be the precursor to another outcome: that men and women will one day—having been cleansed through Jesus' death on a cross—be able themselves to be filled with God.

But before any of that, here at the Jordan Jesus himself is empowered by God as the Holy Spirit comes upon him. Even Jesus does nothing until this has happened; the one who will one day baptise men and women in the Holy Spirit is himself immersed in God.

1. **Mark 1.4-8**

    It has been many years since the people have heard preaching like this. What is different about it? Why do the crowds respond as they do?

2. What is the significance of John's camel hair clothing (Zechariah 13.4), his leather belt (2 Kings 1.8), and his diet of locusts and wild honey (Leviticus 11.22)?

3. **Malachi 4.**

    As the Old Testament comes to a close, who will Israel now be waiting for?

4. There is a famous painting by Grünewald in which John is depicted pointing towards Jesus with an outsized forefinger. Why is this an appropriate way of summarising John's ministry? How might this aspect of Christian ministry sometimes get overlooked today?

5. How do we make sure our ministry is one of pointing to Jesus?

6. Why does Mark tell us about the role Jesus will have as baptiser in the Holy Spirit but not what is achieved on the cross? Which is more important?

• 3

JESUS PREPARES FOR HIS MINISTRY

MARK 1.9 - 13

We read in Kings, Chronicles and elsewhere how Israel repeatedly pursued the same familiar cycle: falling into sin and becoming vulnerable to attack, then crying out to God who would raise up a prophet/king/warrior resulting in victory and revival, only for Israel to fall into sin again. Isaiah the prophet lamented this repetitive pattern and through his prophetic ministry we hear God declaring, '...I was appalled that no-one gave support; so my own arm achieved salvation for me,...'[9] God looked for a faithful Israel to use in his purposes but found a nation in apostasy and unfaithfulness to their call and purpose. Isaiah desperately continues, in Chapter 64.1, 'Oh, that you would rend the heavens and come down...!'

Fast forward to Mark Chapter 1 and we see God's answer to Isaiah's archaic plea: the heavens are now torn open and God's voice speaks, affirming Jesus in his sonship and call, while the Holy Spirit empowers him by coming upon him. The heavens have been rent and God has come down, breaking in to empower a new radical and sacrificial ministry.

---

[9] Isaiah 63.5

The Holy Spirit comes to Jesus in the form of a dove, which popularly symbolises gentleness and peace. Yet the Kingdom of God can also be upsetting and unexpected, and is always dynamic. It is the more forceful aspect of God's Kingdom that is indicated here, and indeed Jesus' own destiny. For his body will one day be broken on the cross, just as the pigeons, or doves, given to the high priest by Mary and Joseph in Jesus' infancy, were sacrificially torn in two.[10]

First, though, God's words to Jesus through the rent heavens anticipate the nature of his personal ministry during the years before he reaches Jerusalem and the cross: 'You are my Son whom I love, with whom I am well pleased.'

The son whom God loves appears in Psalm 2—the one who is God's answer to those who oppose him; the king with authority over nations. Meanwhile the one with whom he is well pleased is the servant-hearted man from Isaiah 42: the one chosen, on whom the Spirit rests and who—yielded to his father's will—brings him delight.[11] Jesus will indeed be a king, carrying authority and yet remaining humble. A servant–king.

Immediately following this moment where Jesus encounters God and understands at least something of what he has been called to, he is sent out by the Spirit into the wilderness where he will be sorely tempted. God's voice to him was of a loving father, though that love does not seek to protect him from the challenge of encountering Satan face to face.

---

[10] See *The Lamb and the Dove*, a The Way of the Spirit short course by John McKay, for a study on this passage and how it relates to Jesus' call and ours.
[11] Isaiah 42.1-4

We read that at the end of his time in the wilderness Jesus is attended by angels and is in the company of wild animals. We are left to wonder whether this scene is perhaps a snapshot of the return of Eden and therefore a further clue as to the purpose of Jesus' ministry which will unfold through the rest of the scroll. It is ambiguous whether the animals are threatening him or simply with him.

Already we are learning that Mark doesn't say everything he wants to explicitly; it is when we dig a little below the surface of the text that we see most.

1. **Mark 1.9–13**

   What does it mean that heaven is torn open? Do we see this happening anywhere else in the Bible? What sorts of things happen when it does? What happens here?

2. **Isaiah 64**

   Israel has waited several hundred years before God answers Isaiah's prayer. What does this chapter tell us about the magnitude of what is about to happen in and through Jesus' ministry?

3. **Leviticus 1.14–17, Luke 2.22–24**

   How might the Holy Spirit coming on Jesus as a dove relate to his calling?

4. We know God is love, and that he is good and kind. In these passages we also see a dynamic Kingdom breaking in, and bloody sacrifice. How might these contrasting Biblical realities help us to hold on to a real view of what it means to follow Jesus?

5. What will Jesus' ministry ultimately achieve? What hope do we find in Mark 1.9–13?

❯ GALILEAN MINISTRY

MARK 1.14 - 8.21

WEEKS 4 - 11

4

REPENT AND BELIEVE

MARK 1.14 - 18

We discover something of Jesus' identity very early on in the Gospel: he is the Messiah and the Son of God.[12] Before we leap to wrong conclusions, though, about what these titles mean, we must remember there had been other messiahs and other sons of God. For 'messiah' simply means 'anointed one', and 'son of God' has been used to describe others in Israel's long history. For instance, King David calls God his father in Psalm 89.[13] (We will see in later weeks what this term might mean for Jesus when he uses it about himself.)

As a messiah, then, Jesus is in a long line of 'anointed ones'. Christians think of him as *the* Messiah in the sense that he was the one who had been specifically anticipated by the prophets, and that God's messianic purpose was fulfilled in his life and ministry.[14] And yet, because his messiahship does not look quite like what either the crowds or his disciples are expecting, the question of who exactly Jesus is runs unanswered right through the Gospel.

---

[12] Mark 1.1
[13] Psalm 89.26
[14] The word 'Christ' is simply the Greek equivalent of messiah, also meaning 'anointed one', and has for shorthand purposes become his surname in the church.

It is not until the end of Jesus' ministry in Galilee, three years on, that Peter exclaims: 'You are the Christ [Messiah]!'[15]

Intriguingly there is a series of clues pointing to an even deeper mystery, one that is never explicitly resolved in Mark, and that is of certain events, statements and actions by Jesus which hint that his identity is bigger than simply that of a—or the—Messiah. Like Peter we need divine inspiration to see clearly, though a working knowledge of the Bible and a desire to dig deep can set us off in the right direction. These clues are hidden between the lines and are hidden away from those who may not be overly familiar with the Old Testament. Even once uncovered, we are left wondering, trying to piece the mystery together for ourselves. When we find these clues, we have the experience of beholding something bigger than we can easily grasp as they tantalisingly hint at an alignment between Jesus and the God of Israel himself, and we are left asking ourselves who he is and how we are to respond to him, today, now.

For now, though, even his identity as the Messiah is something which is still hidden from view for the disciples too, at least up until Peter's great revelation. We may have had the benefit of Mark's hindsight in Chapter 1.1, but the characters in the unfolding drama haven't.

Jesus comes out of the desert preaching a radical message: the time has come; God's kingdom is about to break in. 'Repent, get right with God and believe what I am telling you!' (Author's paraphrase). Jesus has come with the Kingdom, and the action that unfolds will corroborate the insights of Old

---

[15] Mark 8.29

Testament prophets who foresaw God one day interrupting human history again and revealing his glory, this time for the whole world to see.

'Repentance' today is often misunderstood. It may be considered an archaic term, hardly relevant to today's sophisticated Christian world, or it may equally be watered down to mean something like 'being sorry'. It is, however, neither culturally irrelevant nor able to be reduced to simply apologising. It means something very specific: a change of heart, which results in turning around and walking in a different direction.

Now, in Jesus' first sermon, having been equipped at the river Jordan and tested in the wilderness, he tells us how to gain access to God's Kingdom. 'God's Kingdom is so close to you! Repent, Israel—you have been going your own way! Change your heart and turn around—follow me!' (Author's paraphrase). This message is what John the Baptist has been preparing them for and it describes what will be at the heart of Jesus' Galilean ministry: the Kingdom. He will teach the crowds about the Kingdom and train his disciples how to express the life of that Kingdom, equipping them to continue his Kingdom ministry after he has gone. He will demonstrate that the kingdom is not simply a theoretical kingdom, but comes with power and dynamic impact.

So, following 30 years of preparing, Jesus' fast-paced ministry now begins. In contrast to the years of waiting, and the 40 days in the desert, he gets caught up in activity. The opening days of his ministry are replete with forward movement and action. His ministry doesn't begin until he is well into his adulthood, but once it begins its pace is relentless. After his first sermon he begins collecting his disciples, calling them from their day jobs to follow him.

1. **Mark 1.14–18**

    What is the Kingdom of God and how do we access it?

2. What is the difference between the Kingdom and the church?

3. **2 Kings 22**

    What is the difference between repenting and saying sorry? Are you ever guilty of confusing the two?

4.   How did King Josiah act out his repentance?

5.   The disciples have very limited understanding of who Jesus is or why he has come. Why do they leave everything to follow him? Do we need to understand everything in order to follow him?

6.   Many today are encouraged to become Christians by 'inviting Jesus into their hearts'. How does this relate to the response of the disciples? What happened when you became a Christian? Do you need to turn away from anything in order to follow him?

7. **Proverbs 2.1–6, Matthew 16.13–20**

How far can we work out who Jesus is for ourselves, with our own intellect?

5

IMMEDIATE, AMAZING AND WITH AUTHORITY

MARK 1.19 - 28

After Jesus emerges from the desert calling for repentance and proclaiming the coming of the Kingdom, he calls his first disciples: 'Come, follow me!' His ministry has begun, and apart from visits to feasts and festivals about 100 miles south in Jerusalem (which we hear about much more fully in John's Gospel) he now throws himself into busy ministry in and around Galilee. It will be another three years before he will turn and set out for one last journey to Jerusalem, where he will face the authorities and the cross.

The disciples respond by immediately dropping everything, without stopping to count the cost, and following him. Simon, Andrew, James and John are owners of fishing boats and no doubt have invested much effort, time and toil into their fishing businesses; they have much to let go of. Even later, when these disciples become apostles, well known in early Christian circles, the mandate to follow Jesus will not change or even evolve. It is their enduring and unremitting call, as it is ours today, to follow him.

After gathering his first disciples, he goes into the synagogue to teach. We don't know what he teaches but we do see how the people respond. This is typical of Mark: he gives less of Jesus' actual teaching than any other Gospel, but often describes people's responses. Here, they are all amazed at his teaching. They are staggered that there is such an apparent contrast between the teaching of Jesus and those who hold the diplomas and degrees. Those who are most qualified to be teachers are outshone by the man of the Spirit. All we are told about his teaching at this stage is that it is new—and carries authority.

When an evil spirit (rather prophetically as it turns out) cries, 'Have you come to destroy us?' (yes, he has!) Jesus speaks just a few words and the demon has to leave the possessed man. He has not come just to teach, but also to exercise Kingdom authority and power, bringing healing and freedom. God is breaking in afresh through Jesus' life and ministry; the Kingdom he brings is dynamic, potent and effective, and from the beginning impacts people's lives. When the evil spirits call Jesus 'Holy one of God', he orders them to be quiet. He makes no explicit claim to be the Messiah, for he wants the disciples to make their own minds up about who he is.

1.   **Mark 1.19–28**

Note the responses of different people and even of the demonic spirit. How would you explain what is happening?

2.   Can we tell from these verses what Jesus' strategy is going to be? What is it, and what is yours?

3. Note the responses of the crowds. What is different about Jesus' teaching? How is he able to teach with such impact in contrast to the other teachers of the day?

4. How would you have felt about Jesus' ministry if you had been a teacher of the law who had studied hard to qualify?

5. Amid the excitement and activity around Jesus' ministry in Galilee there must also be mystery and uncertainty. How do the disciples cope with that? How do you?

6.   What do you learn from this short passage about the Kingdom? Is Kingdom ministry always like this?

6

REVOLUTIONARY AND EXTRAORDINARY

MARK 1.29 - 2.12

When we read of Jesus rising early to pray, we may recall Isaiah looking ahead to the one who—one day—would be woken morning by morning, listening like one being taught, receiving words that would sustain the weary.[16] Mark now describes Jesus rising early to pray, remaining open to and utterly reliant upon God his Father for all he will need each day.

The concept of God's rule and reign throughout the Old Testament was always one of God concretely breaking in, changing things, restoring and healing; never of some vague, private spiritual experience. Throughout the book of Judges, for instance, we read of the Holy Spirit coming upon certain people at certain times for specific purposes, whether to lead an army or kill a thousand with the jawbone of a donkey. Moses and Elijah saw the power of God's rule and reign manifest in times of specific opposition—Pharaoh and the prophets of Baal respectively. In Isaiah 61, when the Spirit of the Sovereign Lord comes upon an unidentified individual yet to come, it is in order that he will release captives and bind up those who are broken hearted. It is that messianic figure Jesus identifies with, one on whom the Spirit rests and through whose preaching and ministry will come concrete

------

[16] Isaiah 50.4–5

transformations: healing instead of sickness, freedom instead of bondage, life instead of death. He has come for a specific purpose: to set prisoners free.

So, Jesus hasn't come merely to be an amazing teacher or to set a good ethical example, but to walk in the obedience and faith foreshadowed by many through Israel's history. To inaugurate and bring a fuller expression of the Kingdom than has yet been seen, laying hold of God's purposes to see his rule and reign invade and permeate a world which has forgotten its allegiance to the One who created it.

'Let us go somewhere else … so I may preach the gospel there, for this is why I have come.'[17] So Jesus travels, preaching and driving out demons. Filled with compassion for the people, he also heals them—all who humbly come and ask and believe. We see him here responding to the faith of the four friends who carry their friend and lower him through the roof. Miracles of healing point to and give glory to God; they also demonstrate God's kindness, tender-heartedness and love towards the needy.

And already some oppose him.

---

[17] Mark 1.38 – Author's paraphrase

1. **Mark 1.29–2.12**

   Jesus has come bringing the Kingdom of God. What can you learn from this passage about the activities of the Kingdom? List as many as you can, considering how they compare with what we see in our churches today.

2. **Isaiah 42.1–9, Isaiah 61.1–7**

   What do the figures in these two passages have in common? What do they tell us about God's intentions and plans, and his heart towards Israel and, ultimately, mankind?

3.   **Ezekiel 36.16–38**

Isaiah 61.4 talks of restoration, and of rebuilding ancient ruins. Ezekiel uses similar language here. What does it mean?

4.   What hope does Ezekiel offer to Israel, and how do you think—with the hindsight we now have—it relates to the two Isaiah passages, and to Jesus' ministry?

7

INVADING THE STRONGMAN'S TERRITORY

MARK 2.13 - 3.35

Jesus continues to express authority through his teaching and heals all who come to him with faith and expectancy, in stark contrast to the stalwarts at the heart of the religious and political system who are deeply suspicious and find reasons to reject the good news he brings. He continues to build his team, often selecting surprising and even unpopular characters.

As he goes about his Kingdom business he elicits a variety of different reactions, and challenges head on those who interrogate him, parrying their questions by posing his own. He provocatively eats with the marginalised and rejected, permits his disciples to pick and eat grain on the Sabbath and invites a (probably despised) tax collector to join him. He has come with a new wineskin which requires a complete break from the old, and those unable or unwilling to see it just will not get it.

When the Pharisees spy on him and catch his disciples eating the grain on a Sabbath, Jesus reminds them that King David also once ate food that was prohibited.[18] Also like David at one stage in his ministry, Jesus is a king who has already been anointed but whose authority is yet to be recognised. 'You

---

[18] 1 Samuel 21.1–6

are looking at things the wrong way round,' Jesus says. 'The Sabbath was made for man, not man for the Sabbath! You are clinging on to what seemed right yesterday rather than reaching out for and walking in what God is doing today. You have stopped looking for the Creator behind the law—the thinking of your hearts makes you blind.' (Author's interpretation). Their stubbornness, in contrast with the faith of the man with the withered arm, angers and distresses him. This time we see Jesus' reaction rather than the people's!

He takes compassion and heals the man's arm, firing another arrow into the hearts of the religious leaders who are sadly fixated on the letter of the law. The man's faith turns into action as he stretches out his withered arm—the act of faith comes before the miracle happens. The world—then and now—says, 'When I see I'll believe.' Faith says, 'I believe and step out, then I will see!'

The crowds increase and so do the miracles. While all this is happening, Jesus trains his disciples. He teaches them about the Kingdom, demonstrates the Kingdom to them, then sends them out. The first Bible college! Many, including his own family, accuse him, but he must keep moving forwards, for he has come to bring the Kingdom and there is work to do.

1. **Mark 2.13–3.35**

    What is the new wine Jesus wants to pour out? What might a new wineskin look like?

2. What happens when we insist on clinging to the old things?

3. Some are watching Jesus closely (Chapter 3.2). Why? What are their motives? What do they see? What do they fail to see?

4. How does the state of our hearts, including our motives, affect what we see?

5. Why is Jesus so 'deeply distressed'? (Chapter 3.5)

6. Why are the impure spirits able to recognise who Jesus is when the people don't? Why does Jesus order them not to tell others about him?

8

DISCLOSING THE SECRET

MARK 4.1 - 34

The Old Testament prophets rarely spoke of God's 'Kingdom', but often spoke of a vineyard. For instance, through Isaiah Chapter 5 the prophet laments Israel's unfaithfulness: 'My loved one had a vineyard … he looked for a crop of good grapes, but it yielded only bad fruit … for they have rejected the law of the Lord Almighty and spurned the word of the Holy One of Israel.'[19] After lamenting so and God appearing to him in a majestic vision, he is commissioned to go and preach to Israel—a people who will 'be ever hearing but never understanding; be ever seeing, but never perceiving'.[20] He explains he has given them over to their idolatry which in turn has made their hearts hard, rendering them unable to hear or see him. As encapsulated by the Psalmist, they have turned a deaf ear and become like the idols they have turned to.[21]

About 700 years later, despite Jesus pronouncing his mission very clearly, and though many enjoy the miracles and freshness of his teaching, the crowds in Israel remain puzzled and uncomprehending, failing to grasp the significance of the Kingdom he has brought. He teaches in parables, which

---

[19] Isaiah 5.1,2,24
[20] Isaiah 6.9
[21] Psalm 135.17–18

seem to delight them, despite them not (yet) having the key to unlock their meaning and relevance. He seems to speak to his disciples differently though, speaking plainly, not in parables, even suggesting that they already hold the key, though it is not clear that they have much more success than the crowds at grasping the meaning of his teaching.

As Jesus continues to be misunderstood, he urgently encourages them to listen carefully. Though he speaks the secrets of the Kingdom, they aren't unfathomable, and will one day come into the light to be seen by all. With the measure anyone uses to seek to comprehend, he says, they will by that measure find treasure. That treasure, or revelation of the Kingdom, becomes the seed that yields a fruitful harvest—a head of wheat, say, or a very large plant producing shelter for many in its branches. So 'consider carefully what you hear'.[22] Be careful how you listen: dig deep.

In other words, there are mysteries to be discovered by those prepared to search beneath the surface. Just as the veil was drawn back at Jesus' baptism and God's voice was heard, so there is treasure to be found by those who 'call out for insight and cry aloud for understanding, . . . look for it as for silver and search for it as for hidden treasure, . . .'[23] As the people of Israel's hardened hearts eventually blocked them from being able to hear, so there is a new opportunity now in and through Jesus' teaching, and again it is people's hearts that will determine their fruit-bearing potential.

---

[22] Mark 4.24
[23] Proverbs 2.3-4

This first parable Jesus teaches, the parable of the sower, also summarises his vocation: he will sow seed that will only be received by a few, at least during the days of his earthly ministry.

QUESTIONS

1. **Mark 4.1–34**

    Describe the different heart conditions the seed can land in. What needs to happen in our hearts for the seed to bear maximum fruit?

2. Can you recall times when you have left a powerful meeting or group, full of the revelation you have heard, and then something has come in and robbed you of its benefit? Describe what happened.

3. How can you protect yourself from this happening again?

4.   What do you particularly need to guard your heart against?

5.   **Isaiah 5.1–7**

Why is a vineyard a good picture of the Kingdom of God?

6.   **Romans 11.11–24**

What sort of fruit is God looking for from Israel? Now we are grafted into the root, what fruit is God expecting from us today?

7. **Isaiah 6.1–10**

But God doesn't abandon Israel; what does he do?

8. **Proverbs 2.1–8, 3.5, 4.5–7, Mark 4.21–25**

Why don't the people listening to Jesus understand? How can we understand?

9

LIGHT INVADES THE DARKNESS

MARK 4.35 - 6.6

The authority Jesus displayed when he spoke at the synagogue, early in his ministry, is now evident as he confronts chaos, sickness and even death.

The disciples follow Jesus onto a boat and straight into a storm. In the scriptures that Jesus and his disciples would have known, God stills the seas and waves,[24] rebukes the waters and they flee,[25] and in Job is described as the One who set the seas in place and halts the waves.[26] It is God alone who has authority over the waves and all creation. So when, on the boat, the disciples cry out to Jesus and he rouses himself to quell the furious squall, the one digging deeper beneath the surface, searching for hidden treasure, cannot help but line up the figure of Jesus with God himself. The disciples respond in terror and ask themselves who this could be. 'Even the wind and waves obey him!'[27]

When they reach the other side of the lake Jesus reaches out to a Gentile man possessed by an evil spirit. Jesus' Kingdom ministry may initially be

---

[24] Psalm 65.7, 107.28-9
[25] Psalm 104.7
[26] Job 38.11
[27] Mark 4.41

directed towards the Jewish people but through it, we are reminded here, God will eventually bless every nation on earth. The demons have no problem understanding who Jesus is or why he has come, and are cast into a herd of pigs. They are no match for the power and authority Jesus carries.

Back in Galilee Jesus brings Jairus' daughter back to life, and heals a woman who for over twelve years has spent all her savings on doctors who couldn't heal her. In each case he responds not to people's need, but to the faith that they express. He tells the woman directly, 'Your faith has healed you.'[28] We continue to see people responding with amazement and astonishment to Jesus' ministry, though—perhaps with a little wry humour—this time it is Jesus' turn to be amazed, when he is unable to do any miracles in his home town. 'He was amazed at their lack of faith.'[29]

However, as is abundantly clear from his first and foundational parable, that of the sower, not everyone will yet be able to grasp the significance of what he is doing or see beyond the veil to understand the Kingdom he brings. Nevertheless, light continues to invade the darkness.

---

[28] Mark 5.34
[29] Mark 6.6

1. **Mark 4.35–6.6**

    Jesus continues to come relentlessly against the darkness. List the
    different reactions to him you can find in this passage.

2. The woman who has been bleeding for many years reaches out to
    touch Jesus. What is so special about his cloak? What is it that heals
    her?

3. What heals Jairus' daughter? Why does Jesus put out the wailing
    crowd from her bedroom before he heals her?

4. **Psalm 65.5–8, Psalm 104.5–9, Job 38.1–11**

   If you had known these scriptures and seen Jesus stilling the storm in the boat, what might you have concluded about his identity? Would you have thought Jesus' response to the disciples' lack of faith reasonable? (Mark 4.40)

5. What have you learnt this week about what Jesus always responds to? How might our praying change if we were to begin reaching out to him as the woman who is bleeding does? What would that look like in your own life?

- ## 10

SENT OUT

MARK 6.7 - 56

Jesus has barely begun to exercise his ministry but already sends the disciples out, not in the power of the Holy Spirit (Pentecost won't arrive for another two or three years) but in the authority of his name. They preach repentance (turning away from idolatry and back towards God), drive out demons and heal the sick—true Kingdom ministry, just as he himself has shown them. The power at work in their ministry is seemingly no less fruitful than that which is at work in his own.

In contrast with the righteousness of the Kingdom, Herod—even with all his earthly authority as king—becomes trapped in his own murky promises to his alluring stepdaughter. John the Baptist loses his life, marking the end of the line of Old Testament-style prophets. Jesus is bringing something new.

Many Old Testament prophets speak against their religious leaders. Jeremiah, for instance, castigates them for preaching what they think the people want to hear rather than bothering to listen to what God wants to say to them.[30] Ezekiel speaks similarly directly, giving us insight into the

---

[30] Jeremiah 23.9-40

state of the religious system in his day: 'Should not shepherds care for the flock? You have not strengthened the weak, healed the sick, fed the sheep; so I, the Lord, will lead them to good pasture … feed them on the mountains … search for the lost and bring back the strays … I myself will shepherd the flock with justice.'[31]

Jesus is the antithesis of the shepherds of Ezekiel's era. He declines an opportunity to rest, but showing compassion on them (for they are 'sheep without a shepherd') he miraculously provides food for over 5000 hungry people. As if to make a point of identifying with Ezekiel's model shepherd, Jesus doesn't just show that he feeds them but adds the detail, again alluding to Ezekiel, that he sits them 'on the green grass'. He has led them to good pasture.

In a strange sequel, the disciples find themselves struggling to row against high winds as they make their way to Bethsaida, leaving Jesus behind praying on the mountain. He eventually sets off walking on the water and is about to pass them by when, terrified, they cry out to him, as they did on the boat in the earlier storm. Why would Jesus intend to pass them by?

There is a fascinating passage in the Old Testament where Job describes God's strength and majesty in creation and includes the phrase, 'He alone stretches out the heavens and treads on the waves of the sea.'[32] It is God alone who walks on water. A few lines later Job says, 'When he passes me, I cannot see him; when he goes by, I cannot perceive him.'[33] So, God

---

[31] Ezekiel 34 – Author's summary
[32] Job 9.4-8
[33] Job 9.11

'passing by' is describing Job's inability to see, perceive or fathom the extent of God's power and majesty. It is a mystery—it passes him by!

Jesus, treading on the waves and almost passing the disciples by, in the light of Job's words then is a reference to their incapacity to pin down who he is. It is God alone who walks on water (not even a messiah does that!), but since they haven't made their minds up yet about whether he even is the Messiah, any insight or understanding of who he is beyond that is quite impenetrable. The full reality of his identity passes the disciples by too.

1. **Mark 6.7–56**

    What do the disciples do when Jesus sends them out? (Chapter 6.7–13) How are they able to do those things?

2. When God sends us out somewhere, what should we expect to happen? What advantages might we have over the disciples?

3. What leads Herod to behead John the Baptist? What do you think motivates him in life?

4. **Ezekiel 34, Mark 6.30-44**

   Where, in this passage in Mark, do we see evidence of Jesus shepherding in a godly way? How does it compare with the bad shepherds of Ezekiel's day?

5. What does it mean to shepherd God's people today?

6. **Job 9.1-12**

   Use your imagination as you read this passage. What words would you use to sum up God here? Has he changed?

7. **Mark 6.55–56**

Miracles, healings and demons cast out. Faith levels are high. What is the result among the people? What happens as a result of increased faith?

• 11

HEARTS EXPOSED

MARK 7.1 - 8.21

The excitement generated by Jesus' ministry eventually catches the attention of the Jewish leaders in Jerusalem, about 100 miles south, and they travel up to Galilee to see what is going on for themselves. They closely watch Jesus and the disciples, and notice that the disciples fail to keep one of their many ceremonial traditions, that of washing their hands before eating. Of all that is going on in and through Jesus' ministry, this is what they consider of high importance and they duly challenge him about it.

Jesus, unmoved by their allegations, again quotes Isaiah—the passage where he reprimands the Israelites for their hypocrisy in honouring God with their lips, while in reality being a long way from God in their hearts. Jesus adds, 'You have let go of the commands of God and are holding on to human traditions.'[34] Their real problem is not in what they do or don't do, Jesus is saying, but—just as it was centuries earlier with the Israelites of Isaiah's day—is deep within their own hearts. They overcompensate in their external facade for what is missing in their inner lives. Although called to be

---

[34] Mark 7.8

kings and priests,[35] their hearts have grown cold and now focus on legalistic, ceremonial acts.

Jesus has come that they may receive new hearts, and though this will not happen until he has been to the cross, even now he insists it is not those things outside them—other people or circumstances—that destroy them, but only that which is already inside them, in their hearts. Jesus has not come to sort out mankind's behaviour, or to bring a new religion, but to deal finally with the root of the problem.

In stark contrast to the reactions of the Jewish leaders (the ones who might have been expected to applaud Jesus and all he was doing) a Gentile woman openly and spontaneously falls at Jesus' feet, begging him to heal her daughter. Jesus attempts to bypass her requests—after all, he has come first and foremost for his own people—but she insists and her boldness of faith affects him sufficiently that he instantly heals her daughter from afar. Something quite different is coming from this woman's heart than from the religious leaders, unburdened as she is by rules, regulations and other external obligations. Jesus once again responds in accordance with the individual's faith.

For a second time Jesus miraculously provides food from nowhere, the crowds continue to be amazed, and the Pharisees continue to test him. He looks for faith and warns against getting caught by the yeast-like nature of religion and politics. The disciples remain dim.

_____

[35] or 'a kingdom of priests' (Exodus 19.6)

Isaiah Chapter 35 describes what is now unfolding through the coming of the Kingdom. The desert and parched land are becoming glad, bursting into bloom and basking in the glory of God in and through Jesus' ministry. Feeble knees are strengthened, fearful hearts are encouraged, and people's bodies are healed.

1. **Mark 7.1–8.21**

   Where in these passages do we see something other than faith operating in people coming to Jesus? What stops faith from arising in the religious leaders? In us?

2. In what ways can we 'nullify the word of God with our own traditions'?

3. If nothing from outside a man can defile a man, how can we ever blame anyone else or anything else for our response to the circumstances we find ourselves in? Where should we look for the answer in any situation?

4. How can this work for good in our relationships?

5. **Ezekiel 36.24–32, Jeremiah 31.31–34**

    What, according to Jesus, is the relationship between the state of our hearts and our words and actions? What has Jesus come to do?

6. **Isaiah 35.1–10**

   List every fulfilment of this passage you can see in or through the ministry of Jesus. What are the rewards for those who walk this way? When is this fulfilled and who is it talking about?

7. Where are you walking? And with what heart?

JOURNEY TO JERUSALEM

MARK 8.22 - 10.52

WEEK 12

12

SOME SEE, SOME DON'T

MARK 8.22 - 10.52

Everything is about to change: Jesus' Galilean ministry is coming to an end and he will soon begin his journey down to Jerusalem, accompanied by his disciples who, despite Peter's brief moment of insight, remain slow to understand.

The spiritual blindness of the disciples, laid bare by Jesus as he attempts to teach them on their way southwards, is seen all the more keenly as this journey takes place between the healings of two (physically) blind men—the first before they set out from Galilee and the second as they are about to reach their destination.

In case we too are slow to understand what's going on, we must watch the healing of the first blind man at Bethsaida bearing in mind what immediately follows: Peter's revelation that Jesus is the Messiah. When we do this, we see that the two passages strangely mirror each other. For instance, Jesus asks the blind man, 'Do you see anything?' To which he replies, 'I see people; they look like trees walking around.' In the following passage, he asks the disciples, 'Who do people say that I am?' And they reply, 'Some say John the Baptist; others say Elijah; and still others, one of the prophets.' In each case Jesus asks a question and in each case the respondents reply that they see something but foggily, unclearly. The link between physical and spiritual blindness is established.

Peter's recognition that Jesus truly is the Messiah acts as a trigger for Jesus to turn away from Galilee and towards Jerusalem. His messiahship will take on a different character than that which the crowds will be looking for were he to stay. He has enjoyed popularity in Galilee and the crowds have seen the evidences of the Kingdom he has brought, but he must now move towards a very different phase of his ministry. It will be a narrow way indeed to go to Jerusalem, the hotbed of religious and political fervour where many thousands will descend for the coming Passover and where he will face trial and eventually death on a cross. He obediently steps out onto the way ahead, while continuing to prepare the disciples for his departure.

Once immediately after Peter's revelation, and then twice more as they journey to Jerusalem, Jesus teaches the disciples the essence of what it means to be a disciple and three times predicts his own destiny, speaking straightforwardly about what it will cost to follow him. Each time they fail to grasp his meaning.

In the first of the three predictions Jesus refers unashamedly to his imminent death, '... [I] must be killed and after three days rise again ... whoever wants to be my disciple must deny themselves and take up their cross and follow me!'[36] After Peter rebukes Jesus and Jesus in turn rebukes him, he takes three

---

[36] Mark 8.31–34

of his closest disciples, ascends the mountain and is transfigured by the glory of God, attended by Moses and Elijah.

In the second prediction he adds some more detail: 'The Son of Man is going to be delivered into the hands of men. They will kill him, and after three days he will rise.'[37] But they still do not understand what he means, and even argue with each other about which of them is the greatest.

Before he makes his third prediction, Jesus teaches about the rich man wanting to know what he must do to enter the Kingdom of heaven. Maybe, if the disciples could see what Jesus is really saying about the cost of following him, their faces might fall, just as the rich man's does on discovering what the personal cost would be for him to become a disciple. 'Go, sell everything you have and give to the poor, . . . Then come, follow me.'[38] But they are not in the place to hear what Jesus is saying, however clearly he says it. After Pentecost the Holy Spirit will remind and equip them to be able to walk along their own narrow way.

After more teaching and confrontation with demonic spirits comes the third description of what will happen to him in Jerusalem, with even more detail. 'We are going up to Jerusalem, and the Son of Man will be delivered over to the chief priests and teachers of the law. They will condemn him to death and will hand him over to the Gentiles, who will mock him and spit on him, flog him and kill him. Three days later he will rise.'[39] James and John

---

[37] Mark 9.31
[38] Mark 10.21
[39] Mark 10.33–34

approach him and, missing the point, ask if they can have preferential places in glory.

Blind Bartimaeus receives his sight and they approach Jerusalem.

1. **Mark 8.22–10.52**

   What is the difference between the people's expectations of what the Messiah might look like and the reality of Jesus' own calling? Why does Peter suddenly see it?

2. This passage is mainly about spiritual blindness. Can you recall times in your own life when Jesus has tried to say things to you but you have not been able to hear him? What does it say about him that he stayed close to you anyway?

3. How do the disciples' responses to Jesus' teaching contradict what they will one day understand as a call to walk a narrow way? (See Chapters 8.31–33, 9.30-34, 10.32-45)

4. Do you see any of those attitudes in Christians today? In yourself?

5. Imagine you are travelling down to Jerusalem with Jesus and his entourage. Knowing no more than they do, how do you feel? (See Chapter 10.32) Why do you think Jesus is going there?

❯ IN JERUSALEM

MARK 11.1 - 15.41

WEEKS 13 - 15

13

ENTERING JERUSALEM

MARK 11.1 - 12.44

Jesus arrives in Jerusalem on the back of a colt, a sign of royalty (not humility, as is often taught), to the great delight of the massing crowds. Old Testament readers may recall the Psalmist foretelling this scene of people with boughs in hand joining in the festal procession and shouting, 'Blessed is he who comes in the name of the Lord!'[40] As we read that Psalm again we may also notice that the wider context is about a people (or person) crying out to the Lord, experiencing rejection, then paradoxically becoming 'the cornerstone'.[41]

Jesus makes his way towards the temple, which then was a magnificent building whose golden dome dazzlingly reflected the Middle Eastern sun for many miles. From a distance it must have been quite a sight, promising much for the weary traveller approaching Jerusalem from afar. However, when Jesus enters it late in the day, he discovers that it has failed to fulfil Isaiah's prophetic assignment to be a house of prayer for all nations,[42]

---

[40] Psalm 118.26
[41] or in some translations, 'the capstone'
[42] Isaiah 56.7

actually resembling more of a wheeling and dealing centre for all nations, the den of robbers predicted by Jeremiah.[43]

The following day Jesus returns to the temple, and *en route* passes a fig tree. Like the temple, it also looked promising from a distance, but on close inspection it also is found to be lacking fruit—as Jesus discovers when he lifts up its showy leaves. He curses it.

Entering the temple this time, he stops merchandise from being carried through the courts, overturns the merchants' tables, and drives others out. When they next pass the fig tree, they see it has withered from the roots up.

The temple authorities continue to try to catch him out as he challenges them to have faith in God—not a faith that equates to cerebral thought or mental assent, but one that moves mountains. They again challenge his authority but he turns the tables again, so to speak, catching them out with his own penetrating questions and cutting through their rigid religiosity.

They continue to look for things they could use against him, and again and again try to catch him out. Jesus throws their denarius back to them saying, 'Give back to Caesar what is Caesar's and to God what is God's.'[44] Not, manage your money and give a proportion to God, but give God what is due to him: that is, your entire life and heart! For to enter the Kingdom requires a wholehearted turning to the Lord—nothing piecemeal will do. As if to underline the importance of starting from the right place when embarking upon a life following him, he urges the teacher of the law, who

---

[43] Jeremiah 7.11
[44] Mark 12.17

has been listening to the debate, to love the Lord with all his heart, understanding and might.

Unshaken and anticipating what lies ahead, Jesus then reminds the crowd of David's cry in Psalm 110: 'The Lord said to my Lord, "Sit at my right hand, until I have put your enemies under your feet."'[45] This, the most oft quoted Old Testament passage in the New Testament, neatly encapsulates what the early church later understood had happened through Jesus' ministry. That he had—despite what it looked like on the cross—won a titanic, cosmic victory and now sat at the right hand of God, every enemy overcome. Jesus himself speaks this prophetically to those who are opposing his message and his ministry.

As he then tells the parable of the tenants, it can hardly be more clear how he sees himself and what he thinks of the current religious system in Jerusalem. As his Kingdom purpose and ministry is about to lead him onto the most narrow way, towards the cross, he is identifying himself with the beloved son in the parable and understands he is heading towards utter rejection and absolute victory.

Jesus' identity is becoming clear—at least for any who have eyes to see.

---

[45] Mark 12.36

QUESTIONS

1.   **Mark 11.1–12.44**

     Can you see a connection between the fig tree and the temple? Why is Jesus angry? In what ways can religious attitudes cover up lack of fruitfulness, then and now?

2.   **Mark 12.1-12**

     Why does Jesus tell this parable? How does it help us understand what Jesus thinks of his own role and purpose?

3.   How do the authorities react to this parable? Why?

4. **Psalm 118, Psalm 110**

    What do we see of Jesus' ministry foreshadowed in these Psalms?

5. Why do you think the writers of the New Testament quoted Psalm 110 more than any other? What does it tell us of what they believed had happened through Jesus' ministry?

6. To what degree does the church still live in a revelation of Christ's victory won through the cross? To what degree do you?

14

ONE LIKE A SON OF MAN

MARK 13.1 - 37

Elisha's servant awoke to see the King of Aram's army surrounding the city. "'Oh no, my Lord! What shall we do?" the servant asked. "Don't be afraid!" the prophet answered. "Those who are with us are more than those who are with them." And Elisha prayed, "Open his eyes, Lord, so that he may see." Then the Lord opened the servant's eyes, and he looked and saw the hills full of horses and chariots of fire all around Elisha.'[46] The servant was unable to see anything of God's hidden reality, realm and dimension until God himself removed the veil and opened his eyes.

On several occasions in Mark's account we have witnessed such a veil tantalisingly being drawn back: for instance at Jesus' baptism, on the mountain with Peter, James and John, and when Peter momentarily sees who Jesus is. Mysteries, seen and unseen, permeate the Gospel. Mark 13 seems in places very mysterious, notably at the temple and then again on the question of Jesus' identity.

Teaching at the temple, Jesus warns about its impending destruction (which happened in AD70, decades after Jesus' crucifixion). His apocalyptic speech

---

[46] 2 Kings 6.15–17

here looks even further ahead than that, its strange tone and imagery capturing our imaginations but also creating uncertainty as to what and when the events are that are being described. Is he referring to the immediate future, decades ahead, or the end of all time? Certainly, more than one of these are all possibilities, even if somewhat ambiguously intertwined.

Embedded in this apocalyptic teaching,[47] and again later before the high priest,[48] Jesus refers to himself as the Son of Man, having a little earlier quoted also Psalm 110.1: 'The Lord says to my Lord: "Sit at my right hand until I make your enemies a footstool for your feet."' Jesus' understanding of who he is, and what will happen after the cross, is becoming clear. He already anticipates the victory that is about to be won: his destiny is to ascend into heaven, to be led into the presence of the Ancient of Days (the Father), where he will be handed all authority, glory and sovereign power, a dominion or Kingdom that will never pass away.[49]

These Old Testament passages were used much by the first Christians to describe the great victory Jesus had won through his death and resurrection. Today these passages seem as mysterious and hard to grasp with our everyday minds as they were for those listening in Jerusalem. Nevertheless, Jesus urges us earlier in the Gospel to get understanding and to have ears to hear, and so we must dig deep and cry aloud for understanding if we are going to see beyond the veil.

---

[47] Mark 13.26
[48] Mark 14.62
[49] Daniel 7.9-14

The disciples still don't see clearly; indeed, they remain as dull as everyone else! Though Jesus talks to them as if they understand, they clearly, in the main, still do not.

1. **Mark 13.1–37**

    In Jesus' temple sermon, what is he talking about, and when will it take place?

2. How does Jesus begin his sermon? What is the significance of this for us today?

3. What are we to be on our guard against? (Chapter 13.9)

4. Daniel 7.9-14

Here is another apocalyptic passage, with weird and wonderful imagery. Who is the 'one like a son of man, coming with the clouds of heaven'?

5. When do you imagine Jesus first read those verses in Daniel understanding their relevance to him?

6. Psalm 110.1-7

If this is a picture of Jesus arriving in heaven in triumph, where is he today?

7.   How important is it to lift our heads after drinking? What does that
      mean to you in everyday life?

15

SEPARATION, ISOLATION AND HOPE

MARK 14.1 - 15.41

After a woman pours expensive oil over Jesus' head, as a priest might over a king, Judas agrees to betray him and he spends his last meal with his disciples. He then heads for Gethsemane where, in anticipation of the horror of what will follow, he prays that he will be spared his life.

He has entered Jerusalem as royalty, been anointed by a woman, been handed a purple cloak by the soldiers—purple signifying kingship—crowned (with thorns) and mocked, 'Hail, the king of the Jews!' These are mere preliminaries though to his forthcoming enthronement, which is about to take place upon a cross. This is hardly a coronation fitting for a messiah, nor one worthy of Daniel's son of man.

There is a double irony in these last days of Jesus: soldiers ironically treat him like royalty whilst—ironically—he will become the King of all kings. The soldiers little suspect his life and ministry has followed all the scriptural contours of not only a messiah, but *the* Messiah, who will ascend through the clouds into the presence of the Ancient of Days, be given all glory and sovereign power and have dominion over a Kingdom that will never be destroyed.

On the cross, before anyone sees these things, Jesus is mocked and despised by three groups of people, perhaps representing the whole of humanity: the religious leaders, the thieves dying either side of him, and the passers-by (you and me). It has all come to this! The one who stilled the storm, raised the dead, healed and restored wherever he went, is now the one hanging on a cross experiencing a radical and painful separation from all those he knows and loves and—more—even from his Father in heaven. 'My God, my God, why have you [also] forsaken me?'[50] Jesus endures sheer desolation and abandonment by all men and even by God himself. However, though Jesus is experiencing separation from him, God is clearly not absent even from this horrific scene, evidenced by the temple curtain which, at the moment of death, is violently torn in two.

As the temple curtain rips, a different sort of veil, one which has prevented clear-sightedness, is also torn, as Jesus' identity becomes clearer to the Roman soldier observing from the foot of the cross. 'Surely this man was the son of God!'[51] Shockingly, the first revelation of who Jesus is, is to a Gentile, a member of the occupying forces, in anticipation of that revelation going out to all nations.

During his final days Jesus has twice suggested scripture is being fulfilled in and through what is happening, without it being at all clear which specific scripture or scriptures he means. Maybe the clue is in what he himself has said. We have already heard him quote from Psalm 118 about the one

---

[50] Mark 15.34 – Author's interpretation
[51] Mark 15.39

rejected becoming the cornerstone, and, immediately prior to his arrest, from Zechariah about the shepherd being struck and the sheep scattering.[52]

Now we see that he has indeed been rejected, the shepherd struck and the sheep scattered. Not one of the disciples remains at his side as he hangs on the cross. In quoting Zechariah he knew the wider context of that passage, where the prophet tells Judah: 'On that day a fountain will be opened … to cleanse them from sin and impurity.'[53]

The Son of Man is indeed going just as it has been written about him,[54] and scripture is indeed being, and is about to be, fulfilled.[55]

---

[52] Mark 14.27, Zechariah 13.7
[53] Zechariah 13.1
[54] Mark 14.21
[55] Mark 14.49

QUESTIONS

1. **Mark 14.1–15.41**

   What was it about the woman's act of pouring perfume over Jesus that caused the religious leaders such indignation?

2. Judas Iscariot goes to the leaders and they agree together. How powerful is agreement? Which voices are you listening to and agreeing with?

3.   How is Jesus so certain his disciples will fall away? (Chapter 14.27) Peter has great intentions. Why aren't they enough? What else does he need?

4.   When Jesus is mocked and tortured physically, he doesn't react at all. Yet we know he is truly man. How does he do it?

5.   How do you think it feels for Jesus to hang on the cross and suffer rejection not just by those he loves but also by God? How is he able to stay without sin?

6.	What is the significance of the darkness that comes over the scene of the crucifixion at midday?

7.	How is the centurion able to see who Jesus is? How do we see anything at all about Jesus' true identity? When did you first see?

❯ RESURRECTION AND ENDING

MARK 15.42 - 16.20

WEEK 16

16

BELIEVE, GO AND SEE

MARK 15.42 - 16.20

Many themes in Mark come together in these final verses. We saw last week how a Gentile soldier was the first to 'see', signalling the good news now going out into the world and God's glory to be seen by all, not just Israel. All this fulfils Mark's opening verses as he drew on the writings of Isaiah who had foreseen it 700 years earlier.

Joseph of Arimathea boldly asks Pilate for Jesus' dead body and the soldier, a centurion no less, is summoned to a sceptical Pilate. He confirms that Jesus is indeed dead and Jesus' body is released to Joseph who wraps it and places it into a tomb, rolling the stone in front of the entrance. The centurion must be reeling from what he has seen and one wonders whether that is evident in his report to Pilate.

Mary, Mary and Salome see the stone has been rolled away when they visit once the Sabbath is over. They see a young man dressed in white. 'Don't be alarmed,… He has risen!' is the extraordinary news they hear.[56] 'But go, tell his disciples and Peter, "He is going ahead of you into Galilee. There

---

[56] Mark 16.6

96

you will see him, just as he told you.'"[57] Here is another invitation to believe; to put faith into action: go, first, and (then) you will see, second. This is not the way of the world, which always wants to see first before going, but the way of faith.

Trembling and bewildered, however, the women flee and say nothing to anyone.

During his time in Galilee Jesus more than once asked people not to say anything about their healing and they proceeded to go and tell everyone. Here the women are told to go and tell, and this time they don't! What makes these events even more mysterious is that this passage probably formed the original ending of the Gospel. What a strange way to end—in mystery, fear and uncertainty.

Faced with an enlightened Roman soldier, an open grave, an angelic appearance and instructions to 'go', we are left, like the three women, wondering: What do we make of what has happened? How should we react to all that has gone on in Jesus' life and ministry? Have we picked up the clues? Have we called out for understanding and read between the lines? Who then do we say Jesus is?

In the final verses, as the resurrected Jesus meets his disciples on several separate occasions, we hear him still rebuking the disciples for their stubborn lack of faith. Nevertheless (no doubt anticipating Pentecost, when things will become clearer for them), he commands them to go into all creation

---

[57] Mark 16.7

and preach the gospel, assuring them that signs and wonders will follow. Here again, the action of going precedes the signs that will follow. Lift your withered arm and it will be healed; go to Galilee and there you will see me; go into all the world and signs and wonders will follow.

Finally, Jesus ascends into heaven where he sits at the right hand of God.[58] He is the Son of Man who is now given all authority, glory and sovereign power, invited to sit at the Father's right hand until he makes all his enemies a footstool for his feet.[59]

The disciples obey, go, and as they preach, the Lord confirms his word by signs following.[60]

---

[58] Mark 16.19
[59] Daniel 7.13-14, Psalm 110.1
[60] Mark 16.20

QUESTIONS

1. **Mark 15.42–16.20**

    How do you think the centurion feels going to report to Pilate about what he has seen at the cross?

2. The disciples still don't believe. Nevertheless, Jesus commands them to go. How often do preachers preach to where people are at rather than where they should be?

3.   What does Mark's Gospel teach us about faith? How will you apply this in your own life and ministry?

4.   The Gospel is full of descriptions of people's reactions, mainly towards Jesus. What is your reaction to him, having read the whole Gospel?

5.   What is your response going to be? Who do you say Jesus is?

6.	The Gospel ends, despite the strange responses of the women at the tomb and the disciples' unbelief, with a command to go into all the world with the good news. How have you responded to that command? How will you respond with the time you have remaining?

7.	Give thanks for all he has shown you through studying Mark's Gospel!